CW00731555

BIRDS

A PORTRAIT IN PICTURES AND WORDS

BIRDS

A PORTRAIT IN PICTURES AND WORDS

Copyright © Summersdale Publishers Ltd, 2015

Photographs © Shutterstock

All rights reserved.

No part of this book may be reproduced by any means, nor transmitted, nor translated into a machine language, without the written permission of the publishers.

Condition of Sale

This book is sold subject to the condition that it shall not, by way of trade or otherwise, be lent, re-sold, hired out or otherwise circulated in any form of binding or cover other than that in which it is published and without a similar condition including this condition being imposed on the subsequent purchaser.

Summersdale Publishers Ltd

46 West Street

Chichester

West Sussex

PO19 1RP

UK

www.summersdale.com

Printed and bound in China

ISBN: 978-1-84953-675-2

Substantial discounts on bulk quantities of Summersdale books are available to corporations, professional associations and other organisations. For details contact Nicky Douglas by telephone: +44 (0) 1243 756902, fax: +44 (0) 1243 786300 or email: nicky@summersdale.com.

BIRDS

A PORTRAIT IN PICTURES AND WORDS

CHARLOTTE FRASER

summersdale

INTRODUCTION

From the tiny goldcrests that make their homes in our pine forests to the imposing white-tailed eagle, Britain is blessed with an abundance of bird life that takes all shapes, colours and sizes. There's nothing more majestic than watching a swan take flight, or a hawk hunting down its prey; nothing that causes more delight than spotting a friendly robin in your garden or watching the swooping, freewheeling dance of a flock of starlings.

We are a nation of bird lovers, and our feathered friends have long inspired poets, authors, artists and musicians. Izaak Walton called them 'little nimble musicians of the air, that warble forth their curious ditties'. Our stories are filled with wise owls, doves bringing peace, talking ravens and ugly ducklings. It was a skylark that inspired Percy Bysshe Shelley; a thrush for Thomas Hardy: whether big or small, airborne or water-dwelling, each bird has its unique characteristics and charms. Dedicated twitchers and casual admirers alike, we all envy them their power and grace in flight, and listen joyfully to their morning song.

To celebrate birds in all their variety and beauty, this collection of stunning photographs and elegant prose, poetry and quotes offers a full spectrum of our avian friends.

Hear how the birds, on ev'ry blooming spray,
With joyous musick wake the dawning day!

ALEXANDER POPE, FROM 'SPRING'

Yellow wagtail; *Motacilla flava*

He. Where thou dwellest, in what grove,
Tell me Fair One, tell me Love;
Where thou thy charming nest dost build,
O thou pride of every field!

She. Yonder stands a lonely tree,
There I live and mourn for thee;
Morning drinks my silent tear,
And evening winds my sorrow bear.

He. O thou summer's harmony,
I have liv'd and mourn'd for thee;
Each day I mourn along the wood,
And night hath heard my sorrows loud.

She. Dost thou truly long for me?
And am I thus sweet to thee?
Sorrow now is at an end,
O my Lover and my Friend!

He. Come, on wings of joy we'll fly
To where my bower hangs on high;
Come, and make thy calm retreat
Among green leaves and blossoms sweet.

WILLIAM BLAKE, 'THE BIRDS'

Rock dove; *Columba livia*

*God gives every bird its food, but He
does not throw it into its nest.*

J. G. HOLLAND

I was always a lover of soft-winged things.

VICTOR HUGO

Chicken; *Gallus gallus domesticus*

'Summer is coming, summer is coming,
I know it, I know it, I know it.
Light again, leaf again, life again, love again!'
Yes, my wild little poet.

Sing the new year in under the blue,
Last year you sang it as gladly,
'New, new, new, new!' Is it then so new
That you should carol so madly?

'Love again, song again, nest again, young again,'
Never a prophet so crazy!
And hardly a daisy as yet, little friend;
See, there is hardly a daisy.

'Here again, here, here, here, happy year!'
O warble unchidden, unbidden!
Summer is coming, is coming, my dear,
And all the winters are hidden.

ALFRED, LORD TENNYSON, 'THE THROSTLE'

You must not know too much or be too precise or scientific about birds and trees and flowers and watercraft; a certain free-margin, and even vagueness – ignorance, credulity – helps your enjoyment of these things.

WALT WHITMAN

Red-legged partridge; *Alectoris rufa*

It is not only fine feathers
that make fine birds.

AESOP

Oystercatcher; *Haematopus ostralegus*

When cats run home and light is come,
And dew is cold upon the ground,
And the far-off stream is dumb,
And the whirring sail goes round,
And the whirring sail goes round;
Alone and warming his five wits,
The white owl in the belfry sits.

ALFRED, LORD TENNYSON, FROM 'SONG – THE OWL'

Barn owl; *Tyto alba*

Birds… can build and yet leave a landscape as it was before.

ROBERT LYND

Linnet; *Carduelis cannabina*

Lover of swamps
The quagmire overgrown
With hassock tufts of sedge – where fear encamps
Around thy home alone

The trembling grass
Quakes from the human foot
Nor bears the weight of man to let him pass
Where he alone and mute

Sitteth at rest
In safety neath the clump
Of hugh flag-forrest that thy haunts invest
Or some old sallow stump

Thriving on seams
That tiny islands swell
Just hilling from the mud and rancid streams
Suiting thy nature well

For here thy bill
Suited by wisdom good
Of rude unseemly length doth delve and drill
The gelid mass for food

JOHN CLARE, FROM 'TO THE SNIPE'

Pin-tailed snipe; *Gallinago stenura*

Sometimes goldfinches one by one will drop
From low hung branches; little space they stop;
But sip, and twitter, and their feathers sleek;
Then off at once, as in a wanton freak:
Or perhaps, to show their black, and golden wings,
Pausing upon their yellow flutterings.

JOHN KEATS, FROM 'I STOOD TIPTOE'

Goldfinch; *Carduelis carduelis*

Even when a bird walks,
one feels it has wings.

ANTOINE-MARIN LEMIERRE

Thou indeed, little Swallow,
A sweet yearly comer.
Art building a hollow
New nest every summer.
And straight dost depart
Where no gazing can follow.
Past Memphis, down Nile!
Ay! but love all the while
Builds his nest in my heart,
Through the cold winter-weeks:
And as one Love takes flight.

ELIZABETH BARRETT BROWNING, FROM 'ODE TO THE SWALLOW'

Swallow; *Hirundo rustica*

Repeat that, repeat,
Cuckoo, bird, and open ear wells,
heart-springs, delightfully sweet,
With a ballad, with a ballad, a rebound
Off trundled timber and scoops of the hillside ground,
hollow hollow hollow ground:
The whole landscape flushes on a sudden at a sound.

GERARD MANLEY HOPKINS, 'REPEAT THAT, REPEAT'

Cuckoo; *Cuculus canorus*

The little owls call to each other with tremulous, quavering voices throughout the livelong night, as they sit in the creaking trees.

THEODORE ROOSEVELT

Little owl; *Athene noctua*

Every bird which flies has the thread
of the infinite in its claw.

VICTOR HUGO

Chaffinch; *Fringilla coelebs*

The opening of the birch leaves is the signal for the pheasant to begin to crow, for the blackbird to whistle, and the thrush to sing; and, just when the oak-buds begin to look reddish, and not a day before, the whole tribe of finches burst forth in songs from every bough, while the lark, imitating them all, carries the joyous sounds to the sky.

WILLIAM COBBETT, FROM *RURAL RIDES*

Pheasant; *Phasianus colchicus*

Thou, Linnet! in thy green array,
Presiding Spirit here to-day,
Dost lead the revels of the May;
And this is thy dominion.

While birds, and butterflies, and flowers,
Make all one band of paramours,
Thou, ranging up and down the bowers,
Art sole in thy employment:
A Life, a Presence like the Air,
Scattering thy gladness without care,
Too blest with any one to pair;
Thyself thy own enjoyment.

WILLIAM WORDSWORTH, FROM 'THE GREEN LINNET'

Greenfinch; *Chloris chloris*

Thou wast not born for death, immortal Bird!
No hungry generations tread thee down;
The voice I hear this passing night was heard
In ancient days by emperor and clown:
Perhaps the self-same song that found a path
Through the sad heart of Ruth, when, sick for home,
She stood in tears amid the alien corn;
The same that oft-times hath
Charm'd magic casements, opening on the foam
Of perilous seas, in faery lands forlorn.

Forlorn! the very word is like a bell
toll me back from thee to my sole self!
Adieu! the fancy cannot cheat so well
As she is fam'd to do, deceiving elf.
Adieu! adieu! thy plaintive anthem fades
Past the near meadows, over the still stream,
Up the hill-side; and now 'tis buried deep
In the next valley-glades:
Was it a vision, or a waking dream?
Fled is that music: – Do I wake or sleep?

JOHN KEATS, FROM 'ODE TO A NIGHTINGALE'

Nightingale; *Luscinia megarhynchos*

The reason birds can fly and we can't is simply because they have perfect faith, for to have faith is to have wings.

J. M. BARRIE

And as we walked the grass was faintly stirred;
We did not speak – there was no need to speak.
Above our heads there flew a little bird,
A silent one who feared that we might seek
Her hard-hid nest.

Poor little frightened one!
If we had found your nest that sunny day
We would have passed it by; we would have gone
And never looked or frightened you away.

O little bird! there's many have a nest,
A hard-found, open place, with many a foe;
And hunger and despair and little rest,
And more to fear than you can know.

Shield the nests where'er they be,
On the ground or on the tree;
Guard the poor from treachery.

JAMES STEPHENS, 'HAWKS'

Linnet; *Carduelis cannabina*

Why keep pets when every wild, free hawk that passed overhead in the air was mine? I joyed in his swift, careless flight, in the throw of his pinions, in his rush over the elms and miles of woodland; it was happiness to see his unchecked life. What more beautiful than the sweep and curve of his going through the azure sky?

RICHARD JEFFERIES, FROM 'HOURS OF SPRING'

Hen harrier; *Circus cyaneus*

In summer showers a skreeking noise is heard
Deep in the woods of some uncommon bird
It makes a loud and long and loud continued noise
And often stops the speed of men and boys
They think somebody mocks and goes along
And never thinks the nuthatch makes the song
Who always comes along the summer guest
The birdnest hunters never found the nest
The schoolboy hears the noise from day to day
And stoops among the thorns to find a way
And starts the jay bird from the bushes green
He looks and sees a nest he's never seen
And takes the spotted eggs with many joys
And thinks he found the bird that made the noise

JOHN CLARE, 'THE NUTHATCH'

Nuthatch; *Sitta europaea*

Earth has few secrets from the birds.

WILLIAM BEEBE

Little egret; *Egretta garzetta*

He clasps the crag with crooked hands;
Close to the sun in lonely lands,
Ring'd with the azure world, he stands.

The wrinkled sea beneath him crawls;
He watches from his mountain walls,
And like a thunderbolt he falls.

ALFRED, LORD TENNYSON, 'THE EAGLE'

Golden eagle; *Aquila chrysaetos*

Breathe low and soft, O wind! breathe low
Where so much loveliness is laid!
Pour out thy heart in strains of woe,
O bird! that in the willow's shade
Sing'st till the stars do pale and fade.

EDWARD YOUNG, FROM 'UNDER THE VIOLETS'

Long-tailed tit; *Aegithalos caudatus*

I would that we were, my beloved, white
birds on the foam of the sea!
We tire of the flame of the meteor,
before it can fade and flee;
And the flame of the blue star of twilight,
hung low on the rim of the sky,
Has awakened in our hearts, my beloved,
a sadness that may not die.

A weariness comes from those dreamers,
dew-dabbled, the lily and rose;
Ah, dream not of them, my beloved, the
flame of the meteor that goes,
Or the flame of the blue star that lingers
hung low in the fall of the dew:
For I would we were changed to white birds
on the wandering foam: I and you!

I am haunted by numberless islands,
and many a Danaan shore,
Where Time would surely forget us, and
Sorrow come near us no more;
Soon far from the rose and the lily, and
fret of the flames would we be,
Were we only white birds, my beloved,
buoyed out on the foam of the sea.

W. B. YEATS, 'THE WHITE BIRDS'

Black-headed gull; *Chroicocephalus ridibundus*

The river was quite near the house not half a minute from the front door, though hidden from sight by the trees on its banks. Here, at the nearest point, there was an old half-dead dwarf oak growing by the water and extending one horizontal branch a distance of twenty feet over the stream. This was the favourite drumming-tree of a green woodpecker, and at intervals through the day he would visit it and drum half-a dozen times or so. This drumming sounded so loud that, following the valley down, I measured the distance it could be heard and found it just one-third of a mile. At that distance I could hear it distinctly; farther on, not at all. It seemed almost incredible that the sound produced by so small a stick as a woodpecker's beak striking a tree should be audible at that distance.

W. H. HUDSON, *HAMPSHIRE DAYS*

I know a falcon swift and peerless
As e'er was cradled in the pine;
No bird had ever eye so fearless,
Or wing so strong as this of mine.

The winds not better love to pilot
A cloud with molten gold o'er run,
Than him, a little burning islet,
A star above the coming sun.

JAMES RUSSELL LOWELL, FROM 'THE FALCON'

Peregrine falcon; *Falco peregrinus*

Hail to thee, blithe Spirit!
Bird thou never wert,
That from Heaven, or near it,
Pourest thy full heart
In profuse strains of unpremeditated art.

Higher still and higher
From the earth thou springest
Like a cloud of fire;
The blue deep thou wingest,
And singing still dost soar, and soaring ever singest.

In the golden lightning
Of the sunken sun,
O'er which clouds are bright'ning,
Thou dost float and run;
Like an unbodied joy whose race is just begun.

PERCY BYSSHE SHELLEY. FROM 'TO A SKYLARK'

Skylark; *Alauda arvensis*

Never look for birds of this year
in the nests of the last.

MIGUEL DE CERVANTES

Jay; *Garrulus glandarius*

*What law, what reason can deny that
gift so sweet, so natural that God has
given a stream, a fish, a beast, a bird?*

PEDRO CALDERÓN DE LA BARCA

Mallard duck; *Anas platyrhynchos*

Birds know themselves not to be at the centre
of anything, but at the margins of everything.

GREGORY MAGUIRE

Ringed plover; *Charadrius hiaticula*

*The desire to fly is an idea handed down
to us by our ancestors who... looked
enviously on the birds soaring.*

WILBUR WRIGHT

Swift; *Apus apus*

O, curlew, cry no more in the air,
Or only to the waters in the West;
Because your crying brings to my mind
Passion-dimmed eyes and long heavy hair
That was shaken out over my breast

W. B. YEATS, FROM 'HANRAHAN REPROVES THE CURLEW'

Curlew; *Numenius arquata*

A bird is three things: feathers, flight and song, and feathers are the least of these.

MAJORIE ALLEN SEIFFERT

Honey buzzard; *Pernis apivorus*

From troubles of the world I turn to ducks,
Beautiful comical things
Sleeping or curled
Their heads beneath white wings.

F. W. HARVEY

Mandarin duck; *Aix galericulata*

Does the bird know, when, through the waking dawn,
He soaring sees below the silvered lawn,
And weary men who wait to watch the day
Steal o'er the heights where he may wheel and stray?
Can he conceive his fee divine to share,
As a free, joyous peer with sun and air,
And pity the sad things that creep below,
Does the bird know?

HELEN HAY WHITNEY, FROM 'DOES THE PEARL KNOW?'

Corn bunting; *Emberiza calandra*

A Bird came down the Walk –
He did not know I saw –
He bit an Angleworm in halves
And ate the fellow, raw,

And then he drank a Dew
From a convenient Grass –
And then hopped sidewise to the Wall
To let a Beetle pass –

He glanced with rapid eyes
That hurried all around –
They looked like frightened Beads, I thought –
He stirred his Velvet Head

Like one in danger, Cautious,
I offered him a Crumb
And he unrolled his feathers
And rowed him softer home –

Than Oars divide the Ocean,
Too silver for a seam –
Or Butterflies, off Banks of Noon
Leap, plashless as they swim.

EMILY DICKINSON, 'A BIRD CAME DOWN THE WALK'

A goose flies by a chart the
Royal Geographic Society could not improve.

OLIVER WENDELL HOLMES JR

Canada goose; *Branta canadensis*

On me to rest, my bird, my bird:
The swaying branches of my heart
Are blown by every wind toward
The home whereto their wings depart.

Build not your nest, my bird, on me;
I know no peace but ever sway:
O lovely bird, be free, be free,
On the wild music of the day.

But sometimes when your wings would rest,
And winds are laid on quiet eves:
Come, I will bear you breast to breast,
And lap you close with loving leaves.

GEORGE WILLIAM RUSSELL, 'REST'

Bearded tit; *Panurus biarmicus*

What wild creature is more accessible to our
eyes and ears, as close to us and everyone
in the world, as universal as a bird?

DAVID ATTENBOROUGH

Rock dove; *Columba livia*

What I saw was just one eye
In the dawn as I was going:
A bird can carry all the sky
In that little button glowing.

HAROLD MONRO, FROM 'THE BIRD AT DAWN'

Ye flowery banks o' bonie Doon,
How can ye blume sae fair?
How can ye chant, ye little birds,
And I sae fu' o care!
Thou'll break my heart, thou bonie bird,
That sings upon the bough!
Thou minds me o' the happy days
When my fause Luve was true.
Thou'll break my heart, thou bonie bird,
That sings beside thy mate;
For sae I sat, and sae I sang,
And wist na o' my fate

ROBERT BURNS, FROM 'THE BANKS O' DOON'

Reed bunting; *Emberiza schoeniclus*

Little trotty wagtail, he went in the rain
And tittering, tottering sideways he near got straight again
He stooped to get a worm and looked up to catch a fly
And then he flew away e're his feathers they were dry

Litle trotty wagtail he waddled in the mud
And left his little foot marks trample where he would.
He waddled in the water pudge and waggle went his tail
and chirrupt up his wings to dry upon the garden rail

Little trotty wagtail you nimble all about
And in the dimpling water pudge you waddle in and out;
Your home is nigh at hand and in the warm pigsty
So little Master Wagtail I'll bid you a good bye.

JOHN CLARE, 'LITTLE TROTTY WAGTAIL'

Pied wagtail; *Motacilla alba*

Birds are the magicians of the nature! They are here, they are there and they are everywhere!

MEHMET MURAT İLDAN

I heard a bird at break of day
Sing from the autumn trees
A song so mystical and calm,
So full of certainties,
No man, I think, could listen long
Except upon his knees.
Yet this was but a simple bird,
Alone, among dead trees.

WILLIAM ALEXANDER PERCY, 'OVERTONES'

Great tit; *Parus major*

These birds seem to have taught man the art of steering, from the motion of the tail, Nature pointing out by their movements in the air the method required for navigating the deep.

PLINY THE ELDER, *THE NATURAL HISTORY*

Do you ne'er think what wondrous beings these?
Do you ne'er think who made them, and who taught
The dialect they speak, where melodies
Alone are the interpreters of thought?

HENRY WADSWORTH LONGFELLOW, FROM 'TALES OF A WAYSIDE INN'

Great crested grebe; *Podiceps cristatus*

On every bow the foules herde I synge,
With voys of aungel in here armonye.

GEOFFREY CHAUCER, FROM *THE PARELEMENT OF FOULES*

Tree sparrows: *Passer montanus*

In order to see birds it is necessary to become a part of the silence.

ROBERT LYND

White-throated dipper; *Cinclus cinclus*

These are the days when Birds come back –
A very few – a Bird or two –
To take a backward look.

These are the days when skies resume
The old – old sophistries of June –
A blue and gold mistake.

Oh fraud that cannot cheat the Bee –
Almost thy plausibility
Induces my belief.

Till ranks of seeds their witness bear –
And softly thro' the altered air
Hurries a timid leaf.

Oh Sacrament of summer days,
Oh Last Communion in the Haze –
Permit a child to join.

Thy sacred emblems to partake –
They consecrated bread to take
And thine immortal wine

EMILY DICKINSON, '130'

Birds of the same feathers flock together,
and when they flock together they fly so high.

CECIL THOUNAOJAM

Starling; *Sturnus vulgaris*

*The bird is powered by its own
        life and by its motivation.*

A. P. J. ABDUL KALAM

Marsh harrier; *Circus aeruginosus*

The lake was now most still, and reflected the beautiful yellow and blue and purple and grey colours of the sky. We heard a strange sound in the Bainriggs wood, as we were floating on the water; it seemed in the wood, but it must have been above it, for presently we saw a raven very high above us. It called out, and the dome of the sky seemed to echo the sound. It called again and again as it flew onwards, and the mountains gave back the sound, seeming as if from their centre; a musical bell-like answering to the bird's hoarse voice. We heard both the call of the bird and the echo, after we could see him no longer.

DOROTHY WORDSWORTH, *GRASMERE JOURNAL*

Raven; *Corvus corax*

Art thou the bird whom Man loves best,
The pious bird with the scarlet breast,
Our little English Robin;
The bird that comes about our doors
When Autumn-winds are sobbing?

WILLIAM WORDSWORTH, FROM 'THE REDBREAST CHASING THE BUTTERFLY'

Robin; *Erithacus rubecula*

High overhead that silent throne
Of wild and cloud betravelled sky
That makes ones loneliness more lone
Sends forth a crank and reedy cry
I look the crane is sailing oer
That pathless world without a mate
The heath looked brown and dull before
But now tis more then desolate.

JOHN CLARE, 'HIGH OVERHEAD THAT SILENT THRONE'

Grey heron; *Ardea cinerea*

A bird piped suddenly, and was still; and a light breeze sprang up and set the reeds and bulrushes rustling. Rat, who was in the stern of the boat, while Mole sculled, sat up suddenly and listened with a passionate intentness. Mole, who with gentle strokes was just keeping the boat moving while he scanned the banks with care, looked at him with curiosity.

'It's gone!' sighed the Rat, sinking back in his seat again. 'So beautiful and strange and new.'

KENNETH GRAHAME, *THE WIND IN THE WILLOWS*

I don't feed the birds because they need me; I feed the birds because I need them.

ANONYMOUS

Tree sparrows; *Passer montanus*

Thou little bird, thou dweller by the sea,
Why takest thou its melancholy voice,
And with that boding cry
Along the waves dost thou fly?

RICHARD HENRY DANA, FROM 'THE LITTLE BEACH-BIRD'

Sanderling; *Calidris alba*

A widow bird sate mourning for her Love
Upon a wintry bough;
The frozen wind crept on above,
The freezing stream below.

There was no leaf upon the forest bare,
No flower upon the ground,
And little motion in the air
Except the mill-wheel's sound.

PERCY BYSSHE SHELLEY, 'A WIDOW BIRD SATE MOURNING FOR HER LOVE'

Blue tit; *Cyanistes caeruleus*

I value my garden more for being full of blackbirds than of cherries, and very frankly give them fruit for their songs.

JOSEPH ADDISON

When icicles hang by the wall,
And Dick the shepherd blows his nail,
And Tom bears logs into the hall,
And milk comes frozen home in pail,
When blood is nipp'd and ways be foul,
Then nightly sings the staring owl,
Tu-whit;
Tu-who, a merry note,
While greasy Joan doth keel the pot.

WILLIAM SHAKESPEARE, *LOVE'S LABOUR'S LOST*

Tawny owl; *Strix aluco*

I heard (alas! 'twas only in a dream)
Strains – which, as sage Antiquity believed,
By waking ears have sometimes been received
Wafted adown the wind from lake or stream;
A most melodious requiem, a supreme
And perfect harmony of notes, achieved
By a fair Swan on drowsy billows heaved,
O'er which her pinions shed a silver gleam

WILLIAM WORDSWORTH, FROM 'I HEARD (ALAS! 'TWAS ONLY IN A DREAM)'

When my hand closed upon thee, worn and spent
With idly dashing on the window-pane,
Or clinging to the cornice – I, that meant
At once to free thee, could not but detain;
I dropt my pen, I left th' unfinished lay,
To give thee back to freedom; but I took –
Oh, charm of sweet occasion! – one brief look
At thy bright eyes and innocent dismay;
Then forth I sent thee on thy homeward quest,
My lesson learnt – thy beauty got by heart:
And if, at times, my sonnet-muse would rest
Short of her topmost skill, her little best,
The memory of thy delicate gold crest
Shall plead for one last touch, – the crown of Art.

CHARLES TURNER, 'THE GOLD-CRESTED WREN'

Goldcrest; *Regulus regulus*

I caught this morning morning's minion, kingdom
of daylight's dauphin, dapple-dawn-drawn
Falcon, in his riding
Of the rolling level underneath him steady air, and striding
High there, how he rung upon the rein of a wimpling wing
In his ecstasy! then off, off forth on swing,
As a skate's heel sweeps smooth on a bow-
bend: the hurl and gliding
Rebuffed the big wind. My heart in hiding
Stirred for a bird, – the achieve of, the mastery of the thing.
Brute beauty and valour and act, oh, air, pride, plume, here
Buckle! AND the fire that breaks from thee then, a billion
Times told lovelier, more dangerous, O my chevalier!
No wonder of it: shéer plód makes plough down sillion
Shine, and blue-bleak embers, ah my dear,
Fall, gall themselves, and gash gold-vermilion.

GERARD MANLEY-HOPKINS, 'THE WINDHOVER'

Kestrel; *Falco tinnunculus*

The blackbird flies with panic,
The swallow goes with light,
The finches move like ladies,
the owl floats by at night;
But the great and flashing magpie
He flies as artists might.

T. P. CAMERON WILSON, FROM 'MAGPIES IN PICARDY'

Magpie; *Pica pica*

Pigeons and crows,
Take care of your toes,
Or I'll pick up my crackers,
And knock you down backwards,
Shoo all away, shoo away, shoo.

ANONYMOUS, BIRD-SCARING RHYME

Rook; *Corvus frugilegus*

My favourite weather
is bird-chirping weather.

TERRI GUILLEMETS

Marsh tit; *Poecile palustris*

The tame hedge sparrow in its russet dress
Is half a robin for its gentle ways
And the bird-loving dame can do no less
Then throw it out a crumble on cold days
In early march it into gardens strays
And in the snug clipt box-tree green and round
It makes a nest of moss and hair and lays
When e'en the snow is lurking on the ground
Its eggs in number five of greenish blue
Bright beautiful and glossy shining shells
Much like the firetail's but of brighter hue
Yet in her garden-home much danger dwells
Where skulking cat with mischief in its breast
Catches their young before they leave the nest.

JOHN CLARE, 'HEDGE SPARROW'

A bird sitting on a tree is not afraid of the branch breaking, because its trust is not on the branch, but on its wings.

ANONYMOUS

Northern goshawk; *Accipiter gentilis*

*Faith is the bird that feels the light
when the dawn is still dark.*

RABINDRANATH TAGORE

A wise old owl sat on an oak;
The more he saw the less he spoke;
The less he spoke the more he heard;
Why aren't we like that wise old bird?

ANONYMOUS, 'A WISE OLD OWL'

　　　　　　　　　Short-eared owl; *Asio flammeus*

I sat in my sunny doorway from sunrise till noon, rapt in a revery, amidst the pines and hickories and sumachs, in undisturbed solitude and stillness, while the birds sing around or flitted noiseless through the house, until by the sun falling in at my west window, or the noise of some traveller's wagon on the distant highway, I was reminded of the lapse of time.

HENRY DAVID THOREAU, *WALDEN*

Bullfinch; *Pyrrhula pyrrhula*

A dark speck falling, the whish of the grand stoop... red drops on a drift of snow.

HENRY WILLIAMSON

Peregrine falcon; *Falco peregrinus*

Surely no child, and few adults, have ever watched a bird in flight without envy.

ISAAC ASIMOV

Snowy owl; *Bubo scandiacus*

I always wonder why birds stay in the same place when they can fly anywhere on earth. Then I ask myself the same question.

If you're interested in finding out more about
our books, find us on Facebook at
Summersdale Publishers
and follow us on Twitter at
@Summersdale.

www.summersdale.com